IRMA AND ME

A Journal of Hurricane Irma

Louis Petrone

The New Atlantian Library

The New Atlantian Library
is an imprint of
ABSOLUTELY AMAZING eBOOKS

Published by Whiz Bang LLC, 926 Truman Avenue, Key West, Florida 33040, USA

Irma and Me © 2017 by Louis Petrone. Electronic compilation/print editions copyright © 2017 by Whiz Bang LLC.

All rights reserved. No part of this book may be reproduced, scanned, or transmitted in any form or by any means, electronic or mechanical, including photocopying, recording, or any information storage and retrieval system, without permission in writing from the publisher. Please do not participate in or encourage piracy of copyrighted materials in violation of the author's rights. Purchase only authorized ebook editions.

While the author has made every effort to provide accurate information at the time of publication, neither the publisher nor the author assumes any responsibility for errors, or for changes that occur after publication. Further, the publisher does not have any control over and does not assume any responsibility for author or third-party websites or their contents.

For information contact:
Publisher@AbsolutelyAmazingEbooks.com

ISBN-13: 978-1945772665 (The New Atlantian Library)

ISBN-10: 1945772662

IRMA AND ME

Index

PREFACE
KEY WEST BIKE AND PEDESTRIAN COORDINATOR RESIGNS. GREAT!..........................*September 1,2017*
LABOR DAY HURRICANE 1935..................................*September 2,2017*
DACA AND IR......................*September 4,2017*
IRMA ON ITS WAY..................................*September 5,2017*
I'M LEAVING DODGE..............................*September 6,2017*
IRMA AN EXPERIENCE..........*September 7,2017*
ATLANTA MAY BE A SECOND DODGE..............................*September 8,2017*
GO WEST, YOUNG MAN.................................*September 8,2017*
WHAT TO CALL TODAY'S BLOGS................................*September 9,2017*
RANDOM IRMA HAPPENINGS......................*September 10,2017*
SITTING OUT IRMA................................*September 11,2017*
I JITTERBUGGED LAST NIGHT................................*September 12,2017*
A RETURN TO NORMALCY WILL TAKE TIME..............................*September 13,2017*
BELIEV...............................*September 14,2017*
I GET MY FIRST SOCIAL SECURITY CHECK TOMORROW................................*September 15,2017*
IRMA AN EXPERIENCE..................*September 16,2017*
MARIA, MARIA, MARIA...MAY MEET A GIRL NAMED MARIA...THE NAME MAY NEVER BE THE SAME....................................*September 17,2017*

ANTI-SEMITISM HAS ANOTHER BROTHER..................................*September 18, 2017*
CASABLANCA / 18 NEW 15 FOR SEX / TEETH WHITENED AND VAGINA REJUVINATION.........................*September 19, 2017*
I'M GOING HOME!...*September 20, 2017*
GOOD TO BE BACK AGAIN.......................................*September 23, 2017*
IRMA AFTER MATH..*September 24, 2017*
AKNOWLEDGMENTS

Preface

Hurricanes are common in the Florida Keys. Not every year, however. They seem to come one or two a year or for two or three consecutive years. Then a five-year break.

I have owned my Key West home 19 years. During that time, I stayed for anything up to a category 2. Not brave enough to remain for a 3, 4 or 5.

Hurricanes affecting the Florida Keys generally begin off the coast of Africa. Come across the Atlantic. Approach Caribbean Islands. If a hurricane does not turn north, it hits the islands and then Florida.

Not necessarily Key West, however.

Hurricanes are fickle. They change direction and speed by the minute.

As Irma was approaching South Florida, it looked like it was heading straight for Key West. Never deviated. Predicted to be a 5 when it hit.

I previously had seen the devastation a category 5 hurricane can wrought. I drove through Homestead in 1952 three weeks following Andrew. The physical damage the same as if an atomic bomb had been dropped. Nothing left standing, except for an occasional wall. Block after block after block.

I also had written in detail several years ago a newspaper article re the Labor Day Hurricane of 1935. A 5, also.

No way was I staying!

Irma and Me

I was not alone. Key West Mayor Cates advised during the aftermath that 20,000 of Key West's 25,000 residents had also left.

The community was under mandatory evacuation.

Irma was expected September 9 or 10. I figured I would get an early start. Left at 4 the afternoon of Tuesday September 5. My game plan was to drive straight north. At that Time Irma was projected to hit Key West and the lower keys. Broadly. Its path thereafter a bit uncertain. However, up through Florida a certainty.

It was 10 that first night and I was tired. Checked into a Pompano motel. I planned on traveling the Florida Turnpike up the center of the State.

Surprisingly, it appeared everyone decided to leave early. Traffic was heavy that first day.

My destination that evening uncertain. Go north, young man! As far as I could!

I write a daily blog. My Life in Key West. A journal, in effect. I decided to continue writing every day and share my escape from Irma, my life as an Irma evacuee, and my return after Irma to Key West.

Ergo, the title Irma and me.

Irma followed me. I went to Atlanta. Far enough north, I thought. After two nights, left Atlanta. Irma heading for Atlanta. Ended up at the home of friends Jean and Joe Thornton in Birmingham, Alabama.

I was not the only evacuee. There were six others and three dogs.

What follows is the story of Irma and me from September 1 to September 24. I have added a Post Irma section at the end to share the condition of Key West and the lower Keys today. Not great, yet.

Travel with me and learn of the traffic, no gas, long gas lines, an attempted intimidation at a gas station, waiting in line to urinate, imposing on people for more than a week who never considered us an imposition, the return trip through the lower Keys, etc.

Enjoy!

- Louis Petrone
Key West, Florida

KEY WEST BIKE AND PEDESTRIAN COORDINATOR RESIGNS ... GREAT!

Posted on September 1, 2017 by Key West Lou

I am rarely excited about the decisions of the Key West City Commission. They make decisions, pass rules and regulations, and then sit in the corner like Little Jack Horner. Each sticking his thumb in the pie and coming up with a plum. Saying simultaneously ... What a good boy am I!

Decisions off the wall. They throw money at everything. Frequently not the solution.

Last year, the Commission hired a Bike and Pedestrian Coordinator. Chris Hamilton. Never met Hamilton. Began to think he was crazy as he got into the job.

The man moved. Earned his salary by making changes. Changes I considered not always good.

Bikes his job. He removed parking spaces and replaced them with bike lanes. He added bike lanes in dangerous places.

The man was pro-bike and anti-car. He forgot we who drive cars worry constantly about hitting a bike rider who with his 5-member family is rolling down a Key West Street. Some of the kids 4-5 years old. Then there is the 60ish woman who probably has not been on a bike in 40 years. She has trouble keeping her ass on the seat and wobbles uncontrollably.

I could go on.

I hope the position remains unfilled. Traffic congestion and parking problems have to be decided at

Irma and Me

one time by a group. Not piece meal. The City may be moving in that direction.

Got to the Chart Room early. Before 5. Wanted to see John about something. My self-phone lost his number.

My game plan was to go from there to bocce. Never made bocce. The Chart Room was too interesting and fun to leave.

Met George. Nice guy. 47. From New Jersey. A software engineer. Could have been an Arts major. Reads everything. Big on Hemingway.

George visits once a year with a group of friends. One a police officer from Red Bank. The officer's police patch hangs on the Chart Room wall. He proudly pointed it out to everyone.

George told me about Pompous Hemingway. A book of sorts by Hemingway. I tried to find it this morning. Could not. George, if you are reading this blog this morning, e-mail me how to find the book in the Comments section. Forget the long number you gave me. Turned out I did not know how to use it.

The new amphitheater is constantly discussed these days. Who to name it after? A person or company pays a fee for the privilege. Normally, very generous.

Several names have been mentioned. Jimmy Buffett one of them.

The anti-Buffett talk is amazing. Many do not want the facility named after him. Hard to understand. Jimmy Buffet is a part of Key West as much as Hemingway and Tennessee Williams.

A local I had never seen before was sitting at the other end of the Chart Room bar. Attractive. Her feet up on the bar stool next to hear. In her slightly inebriated high-pitched voice she was berating Buffett as a choice.

In the very room where Buffett got his start!

Key West has bright stars in many areas of accomplishment. Dr. Cori Convertino is one.

Cori is affiliated with the Key West Art and Historical Society. She is the Curator at the Custom House.

She is a recognized maritime history expert.

Cori recently completed a two-year project. The Flagler Railroad section of the Custom House. Fantastic!

She has been invited to speak at the U.S. Naval Academy September 14-15 at a maritime symposium. Her topic involves Commodore David Porter and his anti-piracy efforts in 1823 which effectively eliminated piracy from Key West waters.

Sally Rand was a famous fan dancer for many years. Even into her 60's. She lived in Key West in the late 1940's and early 1950's.

I met her in 1965. At a convention at Grossinger's in New York's Catskill Mountains. I was attorney for the group holding the conference.

Sally was retained to perform one evening.

I met her the night before at a small cocktail party at the Grossinger residence. At 60, Sally was still beautiful. We hit it off and I spent much time the next two days when not working in her company.

I was unaware she was the lady friend of one of my client's officer staff. A secret friend. They had had a tiff.

Three days following the convention, I received a letter advising my services were no longer required and I was terminated.

A learning experience.

Harvey has displaced one million persons. Forty-four dead. The number will increase as more bodies are found. Beaumont is a community of 120,000 persons. They have no drinking water.

The sadness of it all.

Irma and Me

Irma is on the way. Similar in power to Harvey. Still two thousand miles away. A hurricane already. Expected to be a 4 when it hits in a week. Winds will be 140 miles per hour plus.

Whether it will reach land or turn north up into the Atlantic not yet certain. At this time heading for the Bahamas. Too soon to determine its impact, if any, with the United States.

After Harvey, I am concerned. I have a feeling in the pit of my stomach.

Enjoy your day!

LABOR DAY HURRICANE 1935

Posted on September 2, 2017 by Key West Lou

The weekend, the time. To recall the Labor Day hurricane of 1935. Especially in view of Harvey's ominous presence.

Hurricanes were not named in 1935. Ergo referred to as the Labor Day hurricane 1935.

The force and destruction of Harvey greater in some respects. Less in others. The 1935 hurricane was considered the biggest of the big in the United States up to that time.

The hurricane struck between Long Key and lower Matecumbe Key. Today, mile markers 73-90 on US 1. The people were aware bad weather was out over the Atlantic. However, it was expected to hit northern Florida. Nowhere near them.

The Overseas Highway was being constructed. Six hundred workers in tents and shacks. Less than 200 alive following the hurricane.

It came in as a category 5. Winds 200 mph. Tides 20 feet above normal. Intense.

Four hundred eighty five killed. Overseas Railroad destroyed, never to be rebuilt.

Survivors in their 80's and 90's remain. One described how ferocious the winds were. She said it ripped the skin off peoples' ears and clothes off their bodies. Survivors were without clothes for days.

A rescue train was sent from Miami. An engine and ten cars. Just as the train arrived, the hardest part of the hurricane hit. The ten cars were blown off a bridge and into the water. Only the engine remained.

Irma and Me

Islamorada was obliterated. Nothing left standing.

Irma is on the way. Still way out. Already a hurricane. Expected to be a category 4 when it hits land.

Where is that land? Not yet known. The track has it going just north of Puerto Rico in a northwest trend. At that point, meteorologists not sure. Will either make a sharp right north over the Atlantic. Or, hit Florida or the Gulf.

I am uncomfortable. The track is straight for the Keys if Irma does not turn.

I had business to attend to yesterday morning. Then a quiet lunch alone at Cuban Coffee Queen. Love the place!

Last night a celebration. For Terri. The doctors have determined she can have certain heavy treatments that will hopefully permit her to live.

Terri is up. Rarin' to get back in the hospital. Her expected stay at least a month.

A small dinner party at Tavern 'n Town. Terri, Donna, Art, George and Louis. Fun! A few tears thrown in in-between.

On the way out, I was walking to the garage behind an attractive couple. Early 40's. As we hit the garage, I heard the male half mention to his lady he thought I was stalking them.

I said, "I heard that!" They swiftly turned around. Assured them I was not a stalker. We had an extremely enjoyable conversation. They were from Scotland. I welcomed them to my country and Key West. They love Key West!

Bocce party tonight! Sons and Daughters of Italy. Pizza and drink first. Bocce play following. Italian music in the background.

It's called remembering your roots! Love the people and the event!

Enjoy your day!

TRUMP LOOKED GOOD

Posted on September 3, 2017 by Key West Lou

Brevity my middle name this morning. Sloan coming over shortly. We have a number of things to do.

I do not recall ever saying anything nice about the President. My mind generally has not changed. Yesterday was rare. He was over the top good.

His appearance in Houston, other parts Texas and Louisiana Presidential. Caused a tear on occasion. The people needed him. He was there for them.

Wish he were able to continue being Presidential. It asks too much of him.

Bocce party last night. Arrived late. Group already playing. The Sons and Daughters of Italy. I continue to be glad I joined. Great people!

President Giorgi a first class guy. Chatted with him a while watching his group and he play.

Then to the Chart Room. Packed. Tourists. Knew not a soul. Watched the first half of the Alabama/Florida State game. Hurried home during half time to catch the second half. Number 1 and number 3 ranked teams playing in a season opening game.

The game was not impressive. Alabama won decidedly, but did not show #1 characteristics. Florida State, a disappointment. I have a feeling they will be stronger as the season progresses.

Syracuse, my Syracuse! Won its opening game Friday night. Decidedly. Beat Central Connecticut 50-7. Have not seen a win like that in years!

Irma and Me

Syracuse has not played well for several years. The school's schedule down graded. Nice to win. But against Central Connecticut?

Brewfest a winner! People lined up around the corner of Duval and South Streets waiting to get in. The party on South Beach.

Sponsored by the Southernmost Beach Resort and Sunrise Rotary. One hundred fifty different brews.

The event will continue throughout the Labor Day weekend.

Filled the gas tank yesterday. Price up $.20 a gallon. Not bad in view of the Houston refinery devastation.

I finish with a Eugene O'Neill quote: "Man is born broken. He lives by mending. The grace of God his glue."

Enjoy your Sunday!

DACA AND IRMA

Posted on September 4, 2017 by Key West Lou

Two items of grave concern. Immediate grave concern.

The first is DACA. Trump will advise his decision tomorrow. His decision re Dreamers. Eight hundred thousand in number per official records. Another million unrecorded.

Trump's decision will reflect the nature of his heart. His humanity.

One way or another, he is going to throw them out. Either directly by his own action, or he will pass the buck to Congress to make a decision within six months or out they go.

Passing final judgment to Congress a joke. Congress has been unable to decide much of anything in recent times in six months.

Till Trump's election, the United States was not the type of nation that would throw Dreamers out. Stalin and Hitler would (or have them killed). Not our cup of tea.

Irma. I fear it may be knocking on Key West's door Sunday or Monday. As a category 4. Meteorologists say too soon to tell. However, the tracking lines they issue say yes.

Scary.

Till 3 yesterday, busy.

Up at 6 to get yesterday's blog out. Sloan at 10. A few hours needed for attention to some matters.

One of the problems involved my cell phone and Key West Lou Live. The video show I do daily on Facebook.

Irma and Me

There has been no live video the past few days. The reason being I could not get a clear picture during the last two videos. Cloudy.

Figured it had to be the phone. Sloan played with it. Not the phone. She thought it was the sunlight behind me. I said no. I have done 30 plus videos from the spot and the sun was never a problem.

Took the phone to Verizon in Winn-Dixie. Great people!

The sun the problem. I said no and explained the other videos being ok. Verizon showed me that previous videos were made during late afternoon. The two that were foggy early afternoon. The sunlight created the difference.

Live and learn! Yes, I e-mailed Sloan and told her she was correct.

Then to Publix. Quiet. Unusual. Sunday afternoons generally busy.

Got home at 3. I still had to take the water pill and lie down for 3 hours. Meant no Hot Dog Church for me.

The Duval Loop bus seems to be doing well. I suspect it will change Duval crawling. Instead of going to the bar next door, revelers will now be able to hit and miss as they so desire. Go from Sloppy Joe's to 801, for example.

William Hackley. I have always suspected he was probably a Confederate. His diary is for the year 1856 so it was impossible to ascertain.

I did some digging. Hackley was a Yankee through and through.

He and his family moved to Washington, DC and resided there from 1863-1865 while Hackley worked in the Treasury Department. Following the Civil War, Hackley continued to work for the U.S. Treasury in another capacity. He was put in charge of Confederate State cotton through 1866.

Hackley makes mention in this day's writing that his wife Matilda payed Mrs. Tift for goods bought for her.

Mrs. Tift Mrs. Asa Tift. I wrote about Asa last week. Asa built the Hemingway House in 1851. Owned 14 slaves at the time. Had the 14 slaves build it.

Asa's bust also sits in the special memorial next to Mallory Square honoring prominent Key Westers over the years.

I suggested if present day political correctness was to prevail, the Hemingway House and Asa's bust should be torn down. The House written with tongue in cheek.

In researching Mrs. Tift this morning, I discovered Asa was a big Confederate supporter. He and his brothers financed the construction of a vessel for the Confederacy. When Lee surrendered, Asa and one of his brothers blew the vessel up rather than let it fall into the hands of the Union.

Asa's bust must definitely come down. On reconsideration, perhaps even the Hemingway House.

The stupidity of it all!

As most of you know, my thinking has come full circle. Leave all these monuments, statues, etc. alone. Tearing down something does not change history. History is what it is. Good, bad or indifferent.

Enjoy your day!

IRMA ON ITS WAY

Posted on September 5, 2017 by Key West Lou

Irma is coming. Will it hit Key West? Looks like it. Only God and two weather fronts can prevent the blow.

I hope my prognostication is wrong. I hope the fronts bend Irma northeast and back into the Atlantic.

Yesterday a first. Irma if it hits not due till Saturday. Saw people putting up hurricane shutters yesterday. Normally, a last minute thing in Key West.

What will Louis do? Not certain yet.

I was supposed to drive Terri to Aqua at 5 last night. She was to perform as part of Dueling Bartenders. Got a call at 4. Forget me. Not feeling well.

Ended up meeting the Chart Room's John for a dinner and drinks. We tried 2 cents on Applerouth. That's its name! 2 cents.

Happy Hour dinner menu. Half price.

Dinner less than ok. Staff bouncy happy. Always a smile. Service excellent. Atmosphere cozy.

John and I stopped at Dueling Bartenders afterwards. Caught the last half hour. Tom Luna and Rick Dery performing.

Great entertainment!

Spent yesterday afternoon preparing for tonight's podcast. Tuesday Talk with Key West Lou. Nine my time. A quick half hour of interesting goings on. www.blogtalkradio.com/key-west-lou.

Topics include DACA, three different hurricanes, Megan Kelly a climber, facial recognition replacing credit cards, killer robots around the corner,

Irma and Me

Netanyahu facing possible indictment, the biggest gold discovery in history, and more.

Trump advises his position on DACA today. Rumor has it he will extend six months and leave the final decision up to Congress. Called passing the buck!

Sad part is Congress hasn't decided anything important in six months in years.

Venezuela's President Maduro has requested he be permitted to appear before the UN's Human Rights Council that begins with three weeks of meetings September 11. He has been granted permission and will appear early in the meetings.

Expect a denunciation of the United States. Perhaps even the UN. Maduro will be calling wolf.

I recall a few years ago when Hugo Chavez spoke before the General Assembly. Bush 2 had spoken immediately before or within 2 or 3 speakers of Chavez.

Things were strained between the U.S. and Venezuela at the time. When Chavez reached the podium, he announced the smell of sulfur was overwhelming. He was referring to Bush's time behind the podium and how Bush in reality was the Devil.

A step back in history. Geronimo.

Geronimo was a great Indian chief. When the white man wanted Indian lands, he led the fight against them. Over 20 plus years, he was responsible for the killing of many U.S. Army soldiers and settlers.

Geronimo became public enemy #1. Pursued relentlessly.

Geronimo finally surrendered in September 1886. The U.S. deported him from his homeland in the west. Initially sent him to two different camps in southern States. Finally, resettled him in Oklahoma.

Geronimo saw the handwriting on the wall. He became the good Indian. A successful farmer and convert to Christianity.

Louis Petrone

America accepted him. Its former enemy. Geronimo marched in President Theodore Roosevelt's inaugural parade in 1905.

Enjoy your day!

Louis Petrone

I'M LEAVING DODGE

Posted on September 5, 2017 by Key West Lou

I have spent 26 years with hurricanes in Key West. Left for most. Would never stay for more than a 2. Was hoping track was going to bend. Does not look like it. I am leaving in about an hour. Could not get a plane. Getting in my car and driving straight north. No particular destination in mind.

Plan on writing blog every morning.

I will not be doing my podcast tonight. Need my home line to do it.

To those of you who have written or called, thank you for your concern.

Enjoy your day!

IRMA AN EXPERIENCE

Posted on September 7, 2017 by Key West Lou

Hi! I am alive and well!

An interesting trip. I write to you this morning from my room on the 39th floor of a Marriott in downtown Atlanta.

Irma scared me. Strange because I have been in Key West for years. For some I stayed, others left. Learned you can handle with no trouble up to a 2. The only bad experience was a tropical storm which sat over Key West for a week.

My home was boarded up. I was alone. Power went out. Had flashlights and candles, food, etc. Basically lived in the dark for a week. No way I could leave. The street under four feet of water. I was alone in the dark so long I even lost the capacity to fantasize.

Irma.

Left Key West Tuesday at 4 in the afternoon. Figured I would get a head start. Drove till 9. Stayed over in Pompano.

Had filled the gas tank the day before. Lines long in Key West and up the Keys.

I went alone. Lisa and family opted to wait till Wednesday morning to see how things looked. The tracking lines changed overnight. Enough that only some wind and rain will hit Key West. Miami became the target.

I should have waited till Wednesday morning.

I was up and out of the motel in Pompano at 6 in the morning Wednesday. Needed gas. Thought I was smart. Get to the station early to gas up. Beat the crowds.

Irma and Me

No crowds at the gas stations. Went to five. No gas. Screwed! I needed gas!

Figured I would get on the Florida Turnpike and hopefully be able to get gas at a rest stop. On the way to the Turnpike, I was driving thru what I would describe as an extremely economically depressed area. Cars lined up! Gas!

A mob scene. People actually arguing who was next in line. No order. People filling up cans with gasoline. The scene one of semi-panic.

Filled up and went for the Turnpike. I think the gas was watered or something. Maybe low grade. Sounds stupid!

Traffic bad off and on. Normal traffic. Nothing to do with Irma. Stayed on the Turnpike all the way up thru Florida. Then a route 75 in Georgia.

Traffic horrendous on occasion because of accidents. Close to Atlanta, big city traffic.

I stopped at a Turnpike rest area to gas up. Still had a half a tank. Wanted to be smart, however. The rest area had gas. The lines waiting to gas up horrendous! State police were directing cars into the pumps. From as close as 20 feet away.

I figured a wait time of an hour at least to get gas. Another screw it situation. Decided to drive further. The problem might ease itself. A 100 miles later, no problem. Drove right up to a pump.

People concerned about Irma for 3/4's of Florida. Then, nothing.

I was falling asleep in heavy traffic in the afternoon. Stopped to eat. End of Florida. I was in Frankfort, NY. The USA 50 plus years ago. Small town people. Chatted with some. They knew little about Irma. Just that it was a hurricane that was going to hit South Florida. Concerned not.

Stopped for gas again early in Georgia. No rest areas. Had to get off 75 and drive down a country road to a gas station.

Big station. Long old building. Called the Plantation. A dozen gas pumps in front.

Sort of old, the pumps. I could not figure out where to put the credit card. Went inside. Just what one would expect in countryside Georgia. A lovely lady. Sixtyish. Short and a bit on the pudgy side. Pure white hair tied in a ball in the back. Metal rim round glasses. Rosy cheeks.

I told her I would like $20 worth of gas. She said to go pump it and come in and tell her how much afterwards.

Would you believe! People, gas stations trusting each other! I told her when I gave her my card afterwards how I had never had a similar experience in Florida or New York. She looks at me with the expression .... Are you for real!

Plantation was a nice store. Countryish. Specialty food items. Honey and fruit cake two examples.

I am 82. I do what I want. Learn what I want. Ignore things I consider a pain.

Never used my cell phone as a travel map guide previous to this trip. Went to Verizon before I left and got educated.

Miracle of miracles! Fantastic! Did not even have to look at it. Just listen to the prompts. Wild!

I definitely would have gotten lost a couple of times without it. Especially when dark and six lanes of traffic each way.

Learned I need an eye examination. Seeing was difficult day and night, with and without glasses.

I did screw up, however.

Was 4 blocks from the Marriott. Could see a tall building with Marriott sign on top. Cell phone went dead. I forgot to plug it back in. Streets one way, round, triangular, etc. Took me a half hour to figure out how to get to the hotel. Finally stopped at a W. Doorman said take a right, another right and a third right ... You will be there! I was.

Great concierge service. A great deal for $137 a night. I forgot my room number after breakfast. Old age! Thought I was on the 37th floor. Not. 39th. Went downstairs for a new key. Like the airport. Had to go thru security to get it.

I have been to Atlanta several times in the past. The US Center for Disease is located there. My environmental cases took me here a week at a time to review records.

My game plan is to buy a pair of long pants. I only have shorts. A sweater and sweatshirt also. Cool for me outside. High today 70. Plus, I only have a pair of worn out crocs. Look terrific! No longer a big city man! Definitely from Key West!

Then, I want to go to Carter's Presidential Museum. Passed by it just before phone went dead last night.

Another interesting experience. Men had to wait in line to pee at Florida rest areas. Just like the ladies. 20-30 people lines. Last time I had the experience was when the Carrier Dome opened in the early 1980s and I had to go at the half time of a football game. Difficult to go when you have a guy standing behind you waiting his turn.

I actually enjoyed the trip experience. However, not looking forward to the return trip.

Got to the bar at the Marriott about 11. Needed a few drinks, not food. Met two interesting people. Jennifer and Jim. No relationship. Thirtyish. In Atlanta on business. Bored them with stories for which I apologize.

Jennifer a financial wizard with Pricewaterhouse. Jim a software guru.

Technology and Louis do not go hand in hand. Age the problem. Not brought up mechanically dependent. Barbara just called and said I should use Uber to get around. My phone not set up yet. She walked me thru it. I'm like a little kid! Can't wait to use it!

Thank you to those who wrote and invited me to share their homes. Good people all.

Enjoy your day!

ATLANTA MAY BE A SECOND DODGE

Posted on September 8, 2017 by Key West Lou

Irma a crazy lady! No question going to hit Key West. Atlanta a good possibility. In the cone on the left. Atlanta hotel throwing me out tomorrow. Staying open, but no room for me. Other areas difficult for reservations also. Many Floridians driving north.

I am going west. To Jean Thornton's home in Birmingham. Key West's Golden Girl. Many others also. Sleep on the floor, etc.

Lisa and family leave this morning. Going north.

Robert Marks. You almost got me. The Weather Channel has been shouting South Carolina also. I opted for Jean, a Key West friend at her Birmingham home. My judgment west better than north at the moment. Take care.

Time of the essence. Short blog. Want to get on the road to Birmingham.

Safety to all involved with Irma.

Enjoy your day!

GO WEST, YOUNG MAN

Posted on September 8, 2017 by Key West Lou

"Go west, young man" is attributed to New York Tribune publisher Horace Greeley. He used the verbiage in an editorial in 1865.

Actually, Greeley lifted the phrase from something a John Babasone Lane Soule wrote in 1851.

Neither actually wrote the phrase as presented here. Each had a slight variation.

History behind us, I want you to know this old man went west. I am in Birmingham, Alabama. At the home of Jean and Joe Thornton. Jean the famous Key West Golden Girl.

Both were kind enough to invite me. Worked perfectly. The hotel had no room for me. I could not get a room anywhere else. The cone began to run over Atlanta.

Birmingham is 2 1/2 hours directly west of Atlanta.

Traffic normal Atlanta to Birmingham. Gassed up mid way. Some pumps are empty. Not because of everyone wanting to tank up. I suspect the gasoline is being shipped to parts of Florida badly needing it.

Alabama a beautiful State. Reminds me of upstate New York. Heavy green foliage. Trees. Big. Type of tree different. What I saw today were 30-50 foot high ones not with leaves. Looked like huge Xmas trees with the branch needles stretching upward.

The Marriott Marquis in downtown Atlanta was some hotel. Huge with all kind of niceties.

I have been in Key West too long without getting off the rock. Maybe 8-10 years. People dress differently on the mainland. Long pants and jackets for men. I

Irma and Me

have no long pants or jackets that fit any longer. My only shoes are a worn out pair of crocs. Big toe peeking out on each.

I talk with everyone in Key West. I felt awkward in Atlanta. The big city overwhelmed me for a while. Overcame it soon.

No question, I have become a Key Wester through and through.

A receptionist at the Marriott by the name of Ella busted her ass trying to get me a room. She did get me an extra day which I passed on. I feared I would run into the Miami escapees if I waited a day longer to leave for Birmingham.

A big hotel well run. Makes our Marriott in Key West look tiny. And we have the largest dining room in Key West! Atlanta's could not match Key West in restaurant size.

Marriott's manager is a Sean John. Left him an e-mail complimenting Ella and sharing my thought of what a well-operated facility he ran.

Cheap, too. $137, without tax. I use a Marriott credit card. Got me an upgrade to a semi-suite that was huge. The Concierge Room was outstanding. Breakfast, hors d'oerves, and drinks.

I was on the 39th floor. Could not help thinking what would I do if there were a fire. Reminded me of that movie way back with Paul Newman and William Holden. A high rise on fire and a big party on the roof. The name of the movie might have been Inferno.

I never left the hotel yesterday. Never got to buy long pants and shoes. Did not visit the Carter Presidential Library and Museum. The driving the day before caught up with me. After lunch, fell into bed and slept 3 hours.

Kind of the Thorntons to take me in. And the many to follow tonight and tomorrow. Jean has been cooking ahead in preparation. Meat loaf tonight because it is comforting. Tomorrow, lasagna for dinner. Alabama football in the afternoon.

Joe drinks socially and smokes. I have a friend! Outside on their back porch. No smoking in Jean's house!

Received a telephone call from Marty Leshaw last night. He was sitting on a boat in Santa Clara, California enjoying a drink.

Marty and I were bosom buddies several years ago. Every night out on the town. Would meet first at the Chart Room. Moved on from there.

Marty semi-retired. He has a beautiful home on the intercoastal in Fort Lauderdale. Plus, a fun house on tall stilts which sits in the ocean somewhere. Marty figures Irma will take them both down.

Marty thought it was time to leave. His wife disagreed. Marty left. She stayed. She did not want to leave her son and family. The son's home several blocks inland and she thought it would be safe.

Marty disagreed. It came down to ... I'm going ... you do what you want. She did. She stayed. Hope she and the family get through this well.

This is blog #2 today. I did a short one as I hurried this morning to get on the road.

Enjoy your day!

WHAT TO CALL TODAY'S BLOG

Posted on September 9, 2017 by Key West Lou

A strange day. In the midst of other strange days. Waiting for Irma!

I believe I have finally escaped her. Birmingham appears a safe hideaway. Hope I am not wrong.

I arrived at Jean's home mid-afternoon. We chatted, watched the weather channel, etc. Joe came home and we chatted more.

Their home has a deeply pitched driveway down. More than 45 degrees. All houses the same. One side of the street the driveways go down, the other up.

The homes are built at the bottom of the Appalachian Mountains. Actually near the bottom. So they have that dramatic pitch.

I missed Jean's house. Had to turn around. Cautiously down a driveway. Getting out the problem. My car stalled almost to the top. Wished I had a clutch car at that moment.

Jean and Joe great hosts. Mi casa, su casa the theme.

It was only the three of us last night. Jean cooked a terrific meat loaf dinner. We knocked down drinks before on their outside veranda.

Never really talked with Joe before. An interesting man. He majored in history. Got a Masters in criminal justice. Wanted to be a police officer. Became one. For ten years.

Irma and Me

Then a friend offered him a job with a manufacturing rep company. Big time electrical machinery.

Joe has been with the company 26 years.

A couple of neighbors popped in. Brought brownies, booze, etc. All charming. A heart doctor lives across the street. Has offered two bedrooms. Another neighbor one. Three others, accommodations also.

True Southern hospitality and neighborliness.

My accommodation terrific. I have a large private room with a queen size bed. I share a large bathroom with another bedroom. The bathroom connects the two bedrooms.

Two ladies arrived around 3 in the morning. They are in the other bedroom. With their dogs. We have bonded.

Life goes on for the Thorntons while we are imposing on their lives. Joe is outside at the moment cutting the grass. Jean is working at a charity garage sale.

It is strange sitting here this morning. Knowing that disaster awaits. I am glad I ran. There are those who did not. I worry about them.

Some remained for financial reasons. Others because they only have a bike. The rest hard heads who don't think Irma will be that bad.

I fear for all of them.

Lisa and family were at Cape Coral. When the west coast became the target, they got out. They are in a friend's home in Jupiter on the east coast.

I am nervous for them. Jupiter may still be too close because of the width of Irma.

Talked with them this morning. The trip up went well. Except for Jake who got carsick.

Louis Petrone

There are many things I would like to comment on. The world, Trump, etc. However nothing is of any consequence at a moment like this, except Irma.

My day will not be bad. Actually, very good. This afternoon we will watch the Alabama game together. Following a lasagna dinner tonight, we will all be glued to the TV worrying about friends and homes in Key West.

I find the sadness of all this heavy. I tear up on occasion thinking of what is to come.

Enjoy your day!

RANDOM IRMA HAPPENINGS

Posted on September 10, 2017 by Key West Lou

I feel like a refugee. I am a refugee. Fleeing Irma.

Some random experiences/happenings the past 24 hours. All Irma related one way or another.

The media has pointedly described Irma: A looming apocalypse ... The surge a minor tsunami ... A lawnmower from the sky.

Spent yesterday afternoon watching Alabama/Fresno State. Alabama killed little Fresno State. My hosts Jean and Joe are Alabama graduates and die hard Alabama fans. I was glad for them.

Followed the game up with a nap. Still tired from the drive.

Rose for cocktail hour. Drinks/drinking excellent! Never had a Beefeaters last night, though a giant bottle was waiting for me when I arrived. Margaritas and wine. The wine exceptional.

Dinner a holiday table. Great food. A neighbor prepared lasagna. Another prepared a Texas streetcake. Chocolate. Absolutely delicious! The wine flowed continuously. Joe started things off with a prayer. Called for under the circumstances.

There are only 9 of us here, plus now 3 dogs. Feels like much more. Fortunately, the house is large enough so we neither run into each other and can get a degree of privacy if so desired.

Several slept on sleeping bags and couches last night. Jean had two neighbors who offered private

Irma and Me

rooms and beds. We all opted to stay together in one house. Team spirit.

The Sheriff moved the 460 Monroe County Jail inmates from Stock Island to a facility in Palm Beach County. One hundred twenty five correction officers went with them and will remain with them.

I do not understand why the inmates were moved. The jail imposing stone and brick.

The Sheriff also maintains an animal farm. Many animals. Well taken care of. A place to visit. The animals were moved from the farm to the jail.

If the jail is safe enough for treasured animals, it should have been safe enough for the inmates.

As of 9 this morning, US 1 not flooded. Except for one lane in Islamorada.

The TV channels are not reporting Irma properly. A lot of talk and next to no video re Key West. Everything video wise primarily Miami.

It is obvious there are no TV people in Key West.

TV is trying to fool people. They got caught by those of us in this house. They ran a video of a flooded Key Largo street. Water rolling as far as the eye could see. 2-3 feet. Two streets.

The streets were Duval and Front in Key West.

Gotcha!

Saw a picture on my cell phone of a woman lighting a candle at St. Mary's of the Sea in Key West. Large votive candles. A statue of the Blessed Mother.

The belief is if candles are lit and prayers said asking for relief from a storm, such will occur. I am not being disrespectful, but I have never seen a Key West hurricane avoided by such conduct.

Saw another video of the White Street Pier on Facebook. The Pier totally covered in water. Right up to the rails. Huge waves pouring over the rails. Two Key Westers running around taking videos. Finally, one of them shouted to the other: Let's get out of here ... this place is too dangerous!

The Marriott Beachside opened its doors yesterday or a day before to guests. Minimum rate. The place is packed with those who stayed. Like Mark Watson. The Marriott was built to sustain a category 5.

Mark Watson reported on Facebook yesterday that they had moved him from a first floor room to a third floor one. Sounded ominous.

La Concha is also taking guests. Built somewhere back in the 1920's. Survived over the years. Thought safe.

I have considered Florida's Governor Scott a flaming asshole up to this point. His political/social decisions rarely helpful to the populace in general. Favor the affluent.

He has turned me around. His Irma conduct beyond belief. His actions thought out and necessary. Like ok for a line of traffic to travel on highway shoulders. Move the cars faster!

In prior storms, all traffic lanes move in one direction. The game plan to get people out of danger's way faster. For Irma, one lane kept open going the other way. Fuel trucks. To get needed gasoline to the southern part of the State.

Every conceivable way has been utilized to get people out of harm's way. Buses provided. Sick and elderly removed from their homes to a safe place. Etc.

Reported that police and fire have left. Felt everything conceivable had been done to get people out. I would agree. I do not believe that some police and fire did not remain. My friends e-mailed me that some have remained at the Marriott Beachside.

The Audubon House. On the corner of Whitehead and Greene Streets. Built way back when by a Captain Geiger.

Irma and Me

In 1832, the famous bird painter John James Audubon spent 20 days residing at the house. He discovered 18 new breeds of birds and painted them.

Our little group has some persons purportedly knowledgeable about Audubon in Key West.

The story told is that Audubon would discover the new breed in the morning. Kill it. Stretch it on something so he could paint it. Painted in the afternoon. Cooked and ate the bird for dinner at night.

It was the eating of the bird in the evening that I found extraordinary.

Those of us here are bonding. I am waiting for someone to suggest we have an Irma reunion once a year.

Enjoy your day!

SITTING OUT IRMA

Posted on September 11, 2017 by Key West Lou

Being bunkered down in Birmingham not bad. Joe is off working somewhere in the west. Jean home with us.

We party starting at 5 each evening. Cocktails and then dinner. Alcohol and wine galore. Exceptional food. Stories flow. Laughter prevails.

Not bad.

Miss Key West, however. I can't wait to return.

Jean Thornton our hostess. Savior perhaps a better word. I have a new label for the wonderful Jean. Hostess with the mostest. The Perle Mesta of Birmingham and Key West.

Jean, a continued thank you for your generosity.

Liz. My dear friend Liz. A year older than me. We date. She cooks for me. We do Dueling Bartenders together. We communicate.

Irma on its way! Liz chartered a plane and flew out. Did not even think to call Louis.

For shame!

I am kidding. Do feel forgotten, however. Liz is in her St. Petersburg home. Large and strong. Survived Irma. Power out. She has a supply of ice however and is able to keep certain foods cold.

Linda Grist Cunningham is a retired newspaperwoman. She and her husband now Key West residents.

Linda was in Virginia with her sickly mother as Irma was arriving. Her husband Ed in Key West. He is riding the storm out with Sheila and David in their Key West penthouse. They survived Irma well.

Irma and Me

Linda has prepared an excellent run down on Irma. Irma: "End of day one in Key West. What we know and don't." She also has put together an Irma site: Hurricane Irma Key West.

I plagiarize a bit today. From End of day one. Linda's accumulated facts better than anything I could put together.

Irma hit Key West as a category 4 8:30 Sunday morning. Actual landfall 20 miles up US 1 at Cudjoe Key. One hundred thirty miles per hour.

Key West has water problems. Main line intact. Some branches broken. A boil water warning in effect.

Many trees down. Those still standing bare. Down to the bark. Foliage ripped away.

There are 42 bridges between Key West and the main land. All have to be checked.

US 1 asphalt road surfaces ripped away in certain areas.

Linda's advisory for those who remained in Key West simple. Conserve water, eat sparingly, and be certain to help each other out.

Thank you, Linda. Keep publishing.

Late tonight is Birmingham's time for an Irma visit. Two in the morning. Not bad. A tropical storm or depression. Kid stuff after what other areas have suffered. We will be safe in Jean's home. I will probably sleep through it.

I have complained re the media's lack of coverage. Miami north covered. The Keys, especially the southern ones, forgotten. We are people too! We were hit first and hard. Media reps should have been in Key West.

One of the Irma escapees in our group has family in the Virgin Islands. Hit by a 5. She has been glued to the TV looking for Virgin Island reports in addition to Key West. Zip! Nothing!

I am doing my Key West Lou Live video on Facebook daily. Nothing fancy. Sitting in a chair holding my cell phone out in front of me.

Mostly Irma at this time. A few minutes. Take a look. You will enjoy.

Finally and most importantly. Yes, there is something more important than Irma. Though some may disagree.

Today is the 16th anniversary of 9/11. Our homeland attacked. Three thousand lives lost.

We must never forget. We must remain vigilant.

Enjoy your day!

THIS IS AN ADDENDUM. I JUST VIEWED A VIDEO OF BIG PINE, ETC. DAMAGE FROM JOYCE GOUSE IN UTICA. THE DEVASTATION FAR WORSE THAN I THOUGHT. WORSE THAN ANYTHING I HAVE SEEN IN THE PAST.

I JITTERBUGGED LAST NIGHT

Posted on September 12, 2017 by Key West Lou

I am 82 years old. I have not danced in 20 years. Nor have I jitterbugged in probably 30. I did last night!

This escape Irma thing is full of surprises. The dancing one of them.

Jean subscribes to Pandora. Terrific! We were listening to '40s and '50s music. All of a sudden, Jean started dancing alone. Eventually, everyone. Jean induced me to jitterbug. Oh, the years I have not done it. It came back. Like riding a bicycle. Did some slow dances also.

The evening was more fun that I have had in a long time. Casa Thornton an excellent place to sit out a hurricane!

The wine helped. I who have drunk nothing but Beefeaters for years am deep into wine this trip.

Irma was to pass over Birmingham at 2 this morning. Nothing. I slept with one eye open waiting to hear and see it. Calm this morning. Calm before the storm? Don't know. I have a feeling it may have passed us by.

Our group of refugees has been reduced by two. One couple left for St. Louis. We are now seven.

The neighborhood knows we are here. They bring goodies for us. Birmingham may know. A TV reporter is stopping by at 11 this morning to interview us.

Don't know when I will return to Key West. Bridges ok to last 16 miles which have yet to be inspected. I live

Irma and Me

2 miles up US 1. TV reported a significant part of the highway in that area uprooted. To be fixed today.

There is neither power, water, sewer nor emergency hospital services.

No access permitted till all in order. Hopefully soon.

No question, we are an imposition. Not according to Jean. My friend for life! I will never forget her!

I reported some tree damage on my video show yesterday afternoon. I am going to repeat them and add a few.

The large tree in front of the Tree Bar on Duval gone. The tree in the middle of Pepe's outside dining room suffered a likewise fate. Virgilio's outdoor bar room tree also gone. 2 Cents' huge tree in the back outside dining area fell also.

Chef Boy Ardee. Probably spelled wrong. A big seller. Supermarket shelves were emptied of the product. Turns out, Chef Boy Ardee can be eaten cold.

Many times the old is better and more reliable than the new. The story of landline vs. cell phones.

Few have kept their landlines. Most use cell solely. Only the landlines are working since Irma. Communication from Key West to elsewhere limited to land lines.

Cell phones not working because cell towers are down. May be a while till cell phone service returns.

I do my Tuesday evening podcast via landline. Tuesday Talk with Key West Lou. Can only use my landline in my Key West home.

Ergo, I will not be doing the podcast this evening.

Key West Lou Live continues, however. My Facebook video show. Via cell phone. A few minutes each day. Nothing fancy. Talk about what ever interests me at the moment. Watch if you can. You may enjoy. Facebook's Key West Lou Live.

Louis Petrone

I am out of things to share. My relationship with the outside world limited. I have not left Jean and Joe's since I arrived. We watch only weather channel news on TV.

Enjoy your day!

A RETURN TO NORMALCY WILL TAKE TIME

Posted on September 13, 2017 by Key West Lou

What Floridians are doing at the moment is not normal. One way or another, Irma's effects are upon us.

Normalcy to me will be getting back to Key West. Just permit me to get home. Hopefully to an undamaged or minimally damaged house. I want to live in my home again!

Not that things have not been great in Birmingham. Jean a terrific hostess. An angel taking care of us evacuees. Accommodations out of sight. Great meals. A cheery atmosphere.

I am concerned about Key West itself. Much damage. Key West will return, however.

Returning to Dodge not going to happen today or tomorrow sadly. TV and social media advise 7-10 days. A long time. Hope I can return sooner. Not only to return, but also to relieve Jean and Joe of the burden they have accepted. Taking care of us. No way can this kindness ever be repaid.

Communication remains a problem. Cell phones useless. Cell towers down. No way to communicate in Florida and parts of Georgia. I understand temporary towers are coming in and will help relieve the problem.

Land lines work. Amazing! The old still true. They are working because regulated and mostly underground. Jean does not have a landline. Few

Irma and Me

people I know have a landline. Even if they did, would not know their number. I only take cell numbers down on my phone.

Trump had it right when it came to social media. The only way Irma information has been circulated. On the spot. Quicker than TV.

Jean says spotty cell phone service has begun this morning. She was able to do a cell phone to cell phone call to Key West.

Throughout Florida, people and pets have been evacuated. There is a fowl breed that has benefited, also. Chickens. The chickens that run around Key West streets.

Tourist think them cute. Natives hate them. Germ bearing and dirty.

Key Wester Jayesh Miami was concerned. He is known as the Selfi King. An Indian. Works in the India store in Key West.

He gathered as many chickens as he could. Wrapped them carefully in paper. Only a bit of the tail and the head sticking out. Laid them carefully in boxes. Then drove them north on US 1. Where, I know not.

In the past few days, I have seen TV videos of two separate beach areas where ocean water should have sat. The power of Irma drew the water from the beach far out into the ocean. Only sand and a few rocks visible.

Amazing power!

Of course, the ocean returned. Called the surge.

The USS Abraham Lincoln came into Key West yesterday. A light carrier. Brought in food and other supplies. The Lincoln will remain a while and its personnel will assist in the clean-up.

There has to be one asshole! Always!

I refer to Sheriff Grady Judd of Polk County. He threatened to jail anyone in his County's shelters who had a warrant pending against them. A leave them out to drown attitude.

Note warrants against people include all kinds of traffic citations also. Like you failed to show up in court re a speeding ticket.

His deputies should be out helping people. First responder type activity and not jailing those with warrants pending.

A court order was sought prohibiting the Sheriff from such action. I could not find information re the outcome of the court proceeding.

Jean and her little group of evacuees have acquired a bit of notoriety in Birmingham. A TV reporter showed up yesterday. Talked with us and filmed us. We appeared on local FOX 6 last night.

Amusingly, I received an e-mail from Great Britain's LBC yesterday afternoon. LBC is a London based national talk and phone in radio station. I am scheduled for a call this morning to be interviewed about Irma.

There has to be a subtle tension involved with being an evacuee. One a person is not aware of.

Yesterday around 4, I got tired. Dead ass tired. Could not believe how tired. Slept on a living room chair a couple of hours. Ate a sparse dinner. Immediately followed by bed. Slept like a baby all night. Feel terrific this morning.

Did not drink at all yesterday.

Joe Thornton has not been with us since Sunday. In Austin on business. Returns tonight at 5.

Don't know if we have room for him!

Enjoy your day!

BELIEVE

Posted on September 14, 2017 by Key West Lou

God is in His Heaven, all is right with the world. The Lord knows everything, even before it happens.

He is all merciful.

So why do disasters like Harvey and Irma occur? Wars? Genocides? I could go on.

I believe. Though no longer a Churchgoer. Speak directly to Him. Generally in times of adversity. Rarely to say thank you when things are good.

People believe in different ways.

Which brings me to the story of Jackie Tee and a silver toe ring.

Jackie's first trip to Key West was 20 years ago this month. With her husband, 4 1/2 year old son, and sister. Jackie purchased a silver toe ring. She has worn it for 20 years.

A couple of months ago, she noticed the toe ring was starting to split. Irma hit Key West September 10. That same day, the toe ring totally split. Jackie found the same ironic. Perhaps meaningful.

Jackie has a friend who she describes as a "new age spiritual." Her friend told her to have the ring repaired: Repair the ring, repair the island. The two went together from the friend's perspective.

Jackie is having the toe ring repaired.

As a side note, Jackie has returned to Key West almost annually the past 20 years. She says the island draws her. It does. Many persons.

Some Key West information.

Irma and Me

Wendy's hit hard by the surge. Seven to 10 days before lower Keys residents can return. No power, water, sewer, limited food.

US 1 bridges all ok. Side road bridges not yet tested. Road debris being removed.

Five food drop sites have been established. Food and water was to be available. People went. Only two had food. All 5, no water. People upset. The first rumblings.

Cell phone service spotty. Persons outside the Keys do not seem to understand. Many complaining why relatives and friends in and from the lower Keys do not call them.

Cell phone service went down 3 hours after Irma hit. I read a report which described the event ... Everything went eerily silent.

Social media has been the savior. I now understand why Trump went to it during the campaign and now as President. Facebook especially helpful.

Hardest hit were Big Pine and Cudjoe Key.

No casualties reported through yesterday.

Re-entry for residents and business owners to MM 73 permitted. Islamorada.

Dusk to dawn curfew remains in place.

A few gas stations beginning to open in the upper Keys.

I received a text yesterday from Shavon White. She is a producer at FOX New York City. She required information about Key West, identification of some who stayed, how to make contact, etc.

Trump arrives today to inspect Irma damage. A proper thing for a President to do. My question is why he is not visiting the Keys. Air Force One could easily land at the Naval Base at Boca Chica. A few short miles from Key West in one direction and Big Pine and Cudjoe Key in the other.

We in the Keys are people too! Could use the lift a Presidential visit brings.

Trump is visiting with EPA head Pruitt. There is an irony to the visit. Both have been working hard to cut disaster relief programs from the federal budget.

They arrive today to take bows for doing a great job in the recovery. First Texas, now Florida. When the budget comes up, they will continue to oppose federally funded disaster relief.

Now a Trump/Sessions scenario of which most are unaware.

Recall the federal program that provided surplus military equipment to police organizations. Police organizations included university police/campus police. What is known as Program 1033.

The program was stopped two years ago by Obama.

Trump signed an Executive Order permitting a resurgence of the program. Supported of course by Sessions. Intent being that law and order prevail on college campuses where students have recently become exceptionally rowdy with demonstrations.

The program is delivering to college campuses grenade launchers, armored trucks, pistols, assault rifles, etc.

The militarization of college campuses! Something like 117 already receiving various items.

I find it difficult to comprehend why military equipment is required to put down college demonstrations. The student will view it as police state activity.

I read somewhere that most students graduate with a debt of $37,000. That much money and they have to oppose heavily armed campus police!

Most campus police today are privatized. Bothers me. They lack oversight. Quick trigger fingers in the making.

Irma and Me

Just received a call from Guy de Boer. KONK Life publisher. He was in Homestead. Leaving the Keys! Homestead has cell phone capability. Guy was calling friends to see if ok, where they were, etc.

He is leaving because he needs cell phone capability to run his newspaper. He will be doing it out of Miami for a few days.

Enjoy your day!

I GET MY FIRST SOCIAL SECURITY CHECK TOMORROW

Posted on September 15, 2017 by Key West Lou

I have heard the term southern hospitality my whole life. It is true! This past week proof thereof.

Jean and Joe the most hospitable without question. Opened their home, refrigerator, etc. to us. Jean just took my dirty clothes and threw them in the washer.

They can never be repaid. Nor do they expect it. They will be remembered, however.

Then there are Jean's neighbors. Three full dinner meals prepared. Desserts and breakfast food. Even a few bottles of booze and wine.

All because they were friends of Jean and Joe and felt sorry for us.

Last night's benefactor was Cindy. A cheerful woman. Widowed some 40 years. Prepared Greek chicken and accompanying dishes. Outstanding!

Cindy a diehard Democrat. Hard to find in this Republican state. Very outspoken in her opposition to Trump and Republicans. Loved her!

Cindy was all excited. She told us that tomorrow (today) she would receive her first Social Security check. An event! I recall when I received my first. A return on something you paid for and had to wait a long time to receive.

We ran out of wine at dinner. Eight bottles.

This hurricane evacuation thing is emotional. Very much so. All of us are just coming down. The

Irma and Me

knowledge Irma did not hit Key West as hard as expected, the knowledge that our homes sustained little damage helps.

Peter Petro called me last night. We now have cell phone service. He is the realtor who takes care of my home. I lost 6 trees. Two in front and four in the back. A dented rain gutter. No water damage. House stinks because I left food in the freezer and refrigerator.

Talked with Anna this morning. The roads in Key West itself are open. She is going to the house today to clean out the freezer and refrigerator.

Spoke with Lisa last night. Still in Jupiter. Their home looks ok. From the air. Roof still on.

The family's first report was from two of Ally's girl friends. Note Ally and the girl friends are in the seventh grade and 12 years old. The two young ladies walked over to Ally's house, checked things out and reported to Ally everything looked ok.

There is humor in tragedy.

Mark Watson reported on Facebook this morning that "I got to sleep butt ass naked in a/c ... I lived like a free man!"

Key West has a For Sale column that runs daily on Facebook. Free. Someone from Ramrod Key advertised yesterday ... House for sale free. A picture accompanied the ad. The home totally destroyed. Flat on the ground.

Tragedy without humor, also.

Carol Schreck lives on a 53′ Defever trawler docked at the Key West Yacht Club. The vessel sunk in its slip. Even though Carol and friends securely tied it to posts, etc.

Carol had planned to stay. Her boat strong and properly secured. Fortunate she did not.

The boat began jumping around when Irma hit. A few men from the Yacht Club jumped in the water to further secure it. Could not. The water too rough. Dangerous. Had to get out.

The Garrison Bight Pier is roughly a quarter a mile away across the inlet. Under repair. Carole's trawler has large pieces of concrete jetty material attached or in the trawler which it is assumed came from the Garrison Bight job.

Hers was the only boat to sink at the Yacht Club.

I have a negative comment to retract.

I mentioned a few days ago that people were lighting candles at the St. Mary of the Sea outdoor Grotto. Tradition tells us praying and lighting candles at the Grotto will prevent significant storm damage to Key West.

Many prayed once again. I questioned and doubted.

I have read several reports today where persons attribute the lack of bad damage to Key West to the candle lighting and praying.

Maybe it works. Real devastation was only 16 and 25 miles away in Cudjoe and Big Pine

I plan on visiting the Grotto, lighting a candle and saying a prayer of thanks when I return.

I suspect I will not be leaving till Monday. Perhaps later.

Power presently limited to 16 percent of Key West. Water limited to 4 hours a day. Must be boiled. Medical services available on a very limited basis at the Community College. Hospital still closed. Search and rescue on Cudjoe Key and Big Pine still ongoing. Only food is that government is bringing in. Stores still closed. A few gas stations open. Curfew dusk to dawn continues. Call service spotty. AT&T and Verizon up and running.

Perhaps the worst problem from a practical perspective is the stink. Got a call this morning. Told

Irma and Me

don't hurry home. Key West stinks! Seaweed, fish, garbage and trash all over. Waste Management not able to clean yet.

Cathy Hakola wrote me yesterday. Facebook, I believe. Told an interesting story. I cannot find it this morning to recite in detail and correctness as received.

Her story has to do with ghosts. Key West has several ghost stories. Most probably false. I suspect a couple true.

One of the true ones involves the Gato House which once was a hospital. Now an apartment house.

Cathy a nurse. A nurse who also rented an apartment in the Gato House after the hospital closed.

History tells us the hospital was run by a very dedicated nurse. Well respected by all.

The claim is her ghost still resides in the Gato House.

Cathy was sick. She woke in the middle of the night to discover someone holding her hand and rubbing her arm. A woman. The ghost.

This went on for several minutes. Cathy says she was not afraid. Found the episode comforting. Woke the next morning much better.

Enjoy your day!

IRMA AN EXPERIENCE

Posted on September 16, 2017 by Key West Lou

Irma an experience! No question about it!

Not just the hurricane itself. The peripheral, the tangents. The whole picture.

Dinner the big event of the day for we evacuees at the Thornton home in Birmingham. A lengthy telephone call from a Key West friend this morning and other information I have obtained re Irma.

There is another world besides Irma. Time for me to begin a return to it. Slowly. Ergo, I will write about a couple of non-Irma items.

The friend who made it back to Key West telephoned this morning. Key West not yet ready for people to return. Not unless they can do without electric power, sewers, food, and gasoline. Which means as a practical matter, no air conditioning, toilet flushing, eating, cars to drive, and working generators.

I start with this morning's phone call.

He and a lady friend ran off to Boston. Made their reservations to return to Fort Lauderdale. Plane reservations honored. $99 deal when made. Airline honored the price, also.

They had a hotel reservation in Lauderdale made a week ago. Honored, no gouging.

People trying to return to the Keys who do not have reservations have difficulty getting a room. The hotel permitted them to sleep in their cars in the hotel garage.

My friend rented a car to drive to Key West. No gouging here either.

Irma and Me

    Florida City the re-entry point. They attempted re-entry yesterday. His lady friend is a nurse and medical emergency trained. She has an identification card to that effect. She was going down to help. She was a go. My friend had nothing. They let him through because he was driving her.

    The roads clear and repaired all the way to Key West. From Florida City to Cudjoe Key, debris stacked on side of road and in the center. Anything that could float or be blown. More trees and refrigerators than anything else. Many boats, also. Debris got heavier at Marathon and increased through Big Pine and into Cudjoe Key. Damage more severe between Marathon and Cudjoe Key. Whole houses actually moved from one place to another.

    From Cudjoe Key to Key West, no debris visible anywhere. The trees were bent from the wind. Items did not fly around. Wind significantly less than elsewhere. A reason why is Key West missed the brunt of the storm. Sixteen miles closer and Key West's damage would have been similar to Cudjoe Key and Big Pine.

    In Key West itself, little property damage. Many trees down, however.

    My friend owns a home in Key West. Very minimal damage to the outside of his home. None inside, except the house smelled big time. He opened the windows to get the smell out. His pool water was black. Trees in the pool.

    Adding to the smell was the fact he did not clean out the refrigerator and freezer before he left.

    Few gas stations open. In and on the way to Key West. In Key West, certain gas stations were pumping gasoline from the gas trucks. Not going through the pump.

The two businesses who appeared prepared for Irma were the primary gay bars. Bourbon Street and 801.

He enjoyed the evening with a friend at Bourbon Street. They had air conditioning, alcohol, food and ice. The air probably provided by large generators. The ice delivered.

He told me a large truck showed up in front of Bourbon Street. Dumped bags of ice at the front door. Then went across the street to 801 and did the same thing.

Curfew is from dusk to dawn. Bourbon Street locked its doors at dusk and was not bothered by the authorities.

End of the friend report.

Since the end of the call, I have learned other things which change or may change certain portions of my friend's report. His report through last night. What follows from this morning.

Two people have died and 10 injured as a result of Irma in Key West.

Gasoline. Continues to be scarce.

Sewer treatment facility functioning. Some house toilets backing up, however. Those that have water or a bucket of water are able to flush toilets. Water still a problem.

Power. Remains a problem. From the Seven Mile Bridge to Key West, only 7 percent have electric power. The upper Keys, 30 percent. The power people are giving special attention to Cudjoe and Big Pine which took the worst beating. Overall, there are 300 downed polls which take time to fix.

Airport. Still closed to commercial and general aviation flights. Expected to reopen Tuesday for all flights.

Irma and Me

Food. Old Publix opened for a few hours yesterday. Other Publix and Winn-Dixie in Key West remain closed. Publix in Big Pine opened only a few hours yesterday.

Evacuees. People like me. Though what I report is not how I feel. There is a rising tension being reported. Evacuees want to return to their Key West homes. In spite of the negatives I have reported. They believe officials are too cautious. I do not want to get on the road till I have motel reservations where needed, know I can get gas all the way back. And when I get back, I have power, air conditioning, gasoline, food, etc.

Return date. Just heard US 1 to Key West opens tomorrow. People are being permitted to return even though things still not as they should be.

Some other bits of information.

Key West is located in Monroe County. Monroe County has one of the most stringent building codes in the United States.

Florida's citrus industry took a beating. The loss statewide is estimated at 50-75 percent.

Re-entry stickers are being forged.

A rumor has spread that a truck was found in the Keys full of dead bodies. Not true.

Now to last night.

Dinner at the Thornton's again. Two guests. Dan and Paula. Not related or connected in any fashion. Both Birmingham residents.

Dan an IT person for a hospital conglomerate that has hospitals from Birmingham south to Broward County. He visits Key West 1-3 times a year. Is a good friend of Jean and Joe.

Dan provided the meal. Bags of Mexican food. The dining room table could not hold all the food.

Wine consumption remained consistent. Tequila added. I missed the tequila. I was tired and went to bed early.

Paula joined us. A friend of the Thornton's. Lovely and charming. Never been to Key West.

Dinner tonight at an Italian restaurant. My treat.

I was going to write of other things. The Irma report took too many words. Already over a thousand. I will save the non-Irma news for another time.

Enjoy your day!

MARIA, MARIA, MARIA ... MAY MEET A GIRL NAMED MARIA ... THE NAME MAY NEVER BE THE SAME

Posted on September 17, 2017 by Key West Lou

The most beautiful sound I ever heard: Maria, Maria, Maria ... I've just met a girl named Maria /And suddenly that name / Will never be the same ... Maria!

The West Side Story's music happy. Irma has not been. Now comes Maria. The song resonates. However, Maria may make us unhappy. As unhappy as Irma.

Maria on her way. A Category 3 at the moment. On a path similar to Irma. Could come right over the Keys and Florida. Maybe not. Maria has a slight bend to the east.

Jose in between. The male meaningless. Expected to downgrade to a tropical storm. If it landfalls, probably the northeast coast of the United States.

For some, Keys' living a dream. Paradise. The reason they located here. Irma destroyed the dream for many. The Keys will recover. The time in between will be difficult.

As Irma approached, the issue for many was whether to stay. Significantly more left than stayed.

A woman who stayed regrets her decision. To those returning at this time, she suggests they do not: "To

Irma and Me

paraphrase Sheriff Ramsey, bring enough resources ... to last a week. If you can't do that, then get back in your car and get the hell out. It's not fun. We have no power. It's hot. We're rationing ice, and the water is brown out of the tap ...We wouldn't stay again."

My friend called me again this morning. Continues to be impressed with 801 and Bourbon Street. Air conditioning, ice and free food. Tells me the same person owns both establishments.

He recommended I not return yet. Very little power, no water, little gasoline, sewer problems continue, the smell/stench abominable, air thick with humidity, ATM machines covered, etc.

He told me I misspoke in yesterday's blog re roadside debris. Could be seen all the way to Cudjoe Key, not Islamorada. From Cudjoe to Key West, merely bent trees.

US 1 opened for residents and business people all the way to Key West 7 this morning. Traffic heavy. Flat tires frequent.

US 1 has only one checkpoint. At Florida City.

Side roads apparently a problem. There are 21 side road checkpoints between Marathon and Key West due to unsafe conditions.

Someone reported on Facebook this morning 2 accidents already on US 1. One of the accidents a head-on. One person dead. I have not been able to verify this information.

My admonition. Drive carefully. Do not speed. An extra half hour in getting to Key West will make no difference.

A personal calamity. Pisses me off.

I have a debit card with Bank of America. About four days before I left Key West to avoid Irma, I received a letter from Bank of America advising someone got into a series of card numbers. They were issuing new cards and I should receive one by the 14th. To use it when received. Ok to use old card in the meantime.

Hurrying to leave Key West, I gave the card no thought. Know I had not received the new card as of the date I left.

Took Jean and Joe and my fellow evacuees to dinner last night. First time I have trued to use the card since 9/3. Card no good. The recorded wording something to the effect my number was not registered with them. I tried every which way to get a human to speak with. No luck.

I had other cards to pay for the dinner.

Figured I would run over to a Bank of America tomorrow morning to get a temporary card. No Bank of Americas in Alabama.

I'm doing good!

I cannot talk to a human bank person till Monday morning during bank working hours on the phone.

I have a feeling I will be returning to Key West at some point this week without the card.

Suppose I needed the card? Suppose it was the only card I had? Suppose I was facing a 1,000-mile drive back to Key West without a card for gas and a motel one night?

In view of Irma, someone at the bank end should have made the decision to keep the old cards good at least till the end of the month. It had to be obvious not all would have received the new card before escaping Irma.

Robert and Ally's dog Jake a Jack Terrier mix. Looks and acts like a Jack Terrier. Took a while, but we finally bonded.

Joanna is an evacuee staying with the Thornton's, also. Johanna is a manager at the Audubon House. She has a Jack Terrier mix. Ralphie. Yesterday, I was sitting

Irma and Me

in a chair watching television and he jumped on my lap. Stayed. I rubbed his head, back and tummy of course.

Ralphie and I are friends. He follows me around. Makes me play with him.

I live and learn.

Teddy Roosevelt was fond of Jack Terriers. The White House had a rat problem. Jack Terriers are the natural enemy of rats. Roosevelt had several brought into the White House to live. It was the end of the rat problem.

Enjoy your Sunday!

ANTI-SEMITISM HAS ANOTHER BROTHER

Posted on September 18, 2017 by Key West Lou

Moving on a step at the time. First with world news. Benjamin Netanyahu and Donald Trump both facing possible criminal charges. Birds of a feather.

Netanyahu's wife is reported to be close to indictment.

Netanyahu's son Yair recently made anti-Semitic comments on Facebook. A prominent neo-Nazi leader referred to Yair as "... a total bro. Next he is going to call for gassings." Yair succumbed to political pressure and removed his comments from Facebook.

Prominent families. Affluent and influential. Both screwed up!

The food continues to be excellent at Casa Thornton.

Ever hear of Blue Apron? I had not till last night. Blue provides prepared meals. Sent by mail. Prepared as to ingredients. Food provided and how to fix. Preparation and cooking the responsibility of the purchaser.

The quality of the meal impressed me. The work involving preparation did not. It took Jean and two ladies a half hour of chopping and cooking.

We enjoyed herb crusted rockfish, chicken ragu, greens in oil, and mashed potatoes. Accompanied by fine wine, of course.

Dessert consisted of three different packages of Keebler cookies. Wine accompanying.

Irma and Me

Entrees and dessert opposite ends of the spectrum.

When do I return to Key West? A minimum two-day trip. I am getting all kind of messages from friends there. Stay / go. My decision will be like flipping a coin.

Everyone has water. Dirty water. Boil first rule. Toilets flushing. Water available fifteen miles north to Shark Key.

Gasoline available. No lines.

Power is sketchy. Comes and goes. I have power thanks to my new residence being near the local hospital. Means air conditioning. Impossible to live without in the Keys.

Three problems of concern remain.

Food continues to be limited. The old Publix is open a few hours a day. A limited number of people allowed in at a time. Government officials advise buying a seven-day supply. The alternative for those returning is to bring a one-week supply with them.

Flats galore on US 1. From debris rudiments remaining. Warning is be prepared to change a flat. I have not changed a flat since law school. Either the car will fall off the jack or I will get a heart attack removing the lug nuts.

Interruption: Re power. I had power. Do not have it now. Anna went to clean. Just called. Ninety-five degrees house room temperature.

Final concern is mosquitoes. I am told they are breeding in the pools. Ergo, many mosquitoes. I was told to return with bug spray. Lots. Also advised some are getting sick from the bites. One person said dengue fever. We had a case or two a few years back. I hope we have not returned to the problem.

Mayor Cates was interviewed on TV yesterday. Key West has a population of 25,000. Twenty thousand left, 5,000 remained. Yesterday residents were permitted to return for the first time. Cates anticipated 8,000 would return the first day. I am anxious to see how the returnees make out today and tomorrow.

Good luck contacting Bank of America. On the phone an hour listening to crappy music waiting for someone to pick up at the other end. A national number. I finally hung up. Both Bank of America branches in Key West closed. It is going to take a few days before my credit card problem is resolved.

Maria, Maria, Maria! She's on her way! Almost the same track as Irma took at this point. A Category 3.

Hope it takes that turn north out into the ocean.

Will I ever leave Birmingham? Nice place. Good company. Excellent food. Excellent wine. Jean is at the store at the moment purchasing another half gallon of Beefeaters.

It is embarrassing being an unexpected houseguest this long. Already over a week.

Enjoy your day!

CASABLANCA / 18 NEW 15 FOR SEX / TEETH WHITENED AND VAGINA REJUVINATION

Posted on September 19, 2017 by Key West Lou

Time to lighten up. Things have been too heavy for more than a week. Even an evacuee experiences stress.

Last night an experience. I watched Casablanca with three women. Jean, Joanne, and Ann.

A great love story. Humphrey Bogart and Ingrid Bergman. The ladies cried throughout. Jean and Joanne had seen the film many times before. For Ann, the first time.

They bawled!

A new study recently released. Concerned teen-age sex. When do the kids start having sex? Used to be 15. No longer. Now, 18. Described as 18 being the new 15.

Attributed to parents and children spending more time together. Parents thereby exercising more influence over them.

Michael Robinson I believe is a Key Wester who escaped Irma, also. I do not know him personally. However, his name and picture were familiar.

Robinson reported in Facebook an advertising sign he saw in Miami: Teeth Whitened and Vagina Rejuvenation.

Could both procedures be done at the same time?

Now to the serious.

Irma and Me

Apparently everyone in Key West now has power, except for me and 44 neighbors. Anna called yesterday that my power was not working. Called Peter the realtor who watches over the house and is also a golf course resident. He had power and so did the people on his block.

He checked into it. I was without power. Turns out 45 homes on the golf course are with another electric company or two companies share the responsibility.

The two companies are arguing over who has to pay for the repairs.

I am not returning without power, water not having to be boiled, food and whatever other calamity remains.

Poor Jean. She may be stuck with us for a long time. I had to think before I shared the no power situation with you. I wanted to be sure the reason I have not left is no power, etc. and not that I have become comfortable living with Jean and Joe.

Looks like Key West is getting a pass as far as Maria is concerned. The projection is it will turn north while still in the ocean.

Florida electrical utilities screw the public. This includes our local Keys Energy. Charge for everything (including using a credit card to pay), frequently increase prices in spite of making significant profit.

The electric utilities and their lobbyists have had laws passed guaranteeing they can play fast and loose with customers.

One example involves solar panels. Florida unquestionably a great place for their usage. The power companies can stop a customer from using solar panels during an emergency by merely flipping a switch.

They do. The companies claim to permit the solar panels to operate could be dangerous to those doing power repairs.

For real?

Trump addresses the United Nations General Assembly today. Never know what he is going to say. He will say something that will enrage most. I hope not something like: North Korea, one more test and we will bomb you.

Republicans are taking one last shot at repealing Obamacare. A Graham-Cassidy bill will be introduced to repeal and replace. Similar to the one that went down to defeat in July, except tougher. Takes away even more things.

Congressional passage and the President signing into law has to occur by September 30. Otherwise, 60 votes will be required in the Senate to pass instead of 50.

On this date in 1881, President James Garfield died. He had been shot in the back and arm 80 days earlier at the Washington railroad station. By an unhappy office seeker, Charles Guiteau.

The back bullet was the cause of death.

Actually, it was several medical mishaps. Malpractice by today's standards.

Garfield was on the dirty railroad floor a long time before being removed. During that time, a nearby physician tried to prod the bullet out. Unsuccessfully. Other persons were touching the wound.

Infection was inevitable.

Subsequent to that day, doctors continued to prod with fingers and instruments for the bullet. They prodded on only one side of his back.

An incompetent doctor was put in charge of the President. The doctor who happened to be present at the railroad station when the President was shot. He insisted the bullet was on one side, the side it had entered, and only that side could be prodded.

Clean doctor's hands not a practice at the time.

Irma and Me

The bullet had to be found. It was causing the infection killing the President.

Even Thomas Edison was called in. He had recently invented a new machine that could detect foreign objects in the body. The machine had been successfully tested on numerous Civil War veterans.

The machine could locate nothing.

The reason was the President was laying on a metal spring mattress. The mattress having only recently been invented. One had been given to the White House free for the President's use.

The metal springs screwed up Edison's machine. It did work properly. However not on metal springs.

When Garfield died, it was found the bullet was not on the side of his back where the doctors thought. It was on the other side. The prodding had caused it to move. The doctors were looking in the wrong place.

Guiteau was placed on trial for murder. His defense was he did not kill the President, the doctors did. Technically correct. Never the less, he was found guilty and executed.

I apologize for being long winded re the Garfield story. I wrote a lengthy column several years ago for KONK Life concerning the shooting and the President's death.

No Tuesday Talk with Key West Lou tonight. The podcast requires my landline in Key West to do the show. Enjoy your day!

I'M GOING HOME!

Posted on September 20, 2017 by Key West Lou

Power restored.

I am leaving in about an hour.

No time for blog today. Nor will there be one tomorrow. I will still be on the road.

I cannot thank Jean and Joe enough for their kindness. Was it a musical line …That's what friends are for!

To the who wrote adverse comments about my stay here, what can I tell you. One even called me a leech.

Besides benefiting from the goodness of good-hearted people, I look at it as payback. I have taken in persons in distress many times. Anywhere from 5 days to 6 months. Called do unto others as you would have them do unto you.

To another who criticized, I did more than dinner. That is me.

Then there were those who thought it improper for me to have left. I had a lot of company. Mayor Cates said the population of Key West is 25,000 and 20,000 had left.

Additionally if one could afford to leave, he/she would have been crazy to stay with a then category 5 on the way.

Then there is the burden factor. I am 82 with a bad heart. Cannot walk more than 50 feet without being seriously breathless. I have a balance problem. Fall frequently. There is the tightening in the chest if I exert myself.

This is my last reference to these issues. I am moving on. Hope you will also.

Enjoy your day!

GOOD TO BE BACK AGAIN

Posted on September 23, 2017 by Key West Lou

Stealing from Mac Arthur ... I have returned! Gene Autry ... I'm back in the saddle again!

It is good to be home.

I got in at 4 Thursday afternoon after two days of driving. Birmingham to Key West. Eight hours each day.

No question, a few days does make a difference. Specifically with regard to traffic. Little traffic. Very little. Only spots crowded were Orlando and Miami. I used the Florida Turnpike.

No waiting in line for gasoline. Pumps available at all times.

The second day depressing, however.

I spent all day listening to the radio re the Mexican school collapse and the search for Frida Sophia and perhaps several other children. Drama! Heart wrenching!

Yesterday, we were told by Mexican authorities that there was no Frida or any other children beneath the wreckage. Alive or dead. The situation "not a reality."

There has to be more to the story. Does not make sense to me.

The search for the children weighed heavy. To it was added another sadness. I saw what Irma did to the Keys.

Irma and Me

Beginning with Florida City, a relatively small tree down here and there. Just outside Marathon, you could sense things were going to get bad. They did.

Beginning at the Marathon point and down to Sugarloaf, everything got consistently worse. Debris piled on the side of US 1. Furniture and mattresses. Refrigerators. Boats upside down. Cars on their sides. Roofs off. Buildings down.

Big Pine, an absolute disaster. It was as if King Kong had stomped all over it.

Summerland, Cudjoe and Sugarloaf hit badly, also.

I had been informed I would see many refrigerators. Apparently they fly through the air with the greatest of ease. I even saw one in a tree. A big one. About 15 feet up, laying sideways on a couple of big branches.

The damage itself was too much to take. Coupled with the little girl under the Mexican school, both scenarios combined too much to take. Tears were actually slowly rolling down my cheeks at one point.

Key West was a different story. Damage, yes. A roof gone here and there. Most signs blown through. Trees the real problem. Toppled. Size immaterial. Big and little ones.

My new home is in an area covered with large trees. A cathedral type appearance over the streets.

No more. I was shocked! At least half the trees down. The roads one lane. Piled debris on roadside heavy.

My new home survived. No damage. Except for a big tree and little tree in front and 5 little ones (20 footers) in the back.

I thought I was returning to full services. No Comcast television, computer and landline. All three I discovered have been off since September 7. One day after I left, three days before Irma hit.

Comcast no help. Comcast's attitude always the same. Don't care/don't bother me.

I called to ask when I would get service. The operator did not know. She asked if I was aware there had been a hurricane.

I am getting wi-fi from my cell phone. A special app. Extra cost.

I went out Thursday night. Duval Street a ghost town. Places still boarded. No one on the street.

Met up with John, Kevin and Molly at Bourbon Street. Very few bars open. Food, forget it!

On the way home, I stopped at the Marriott Beachside. Asked for a menu. No food! Enjoyed a drink, met some nice folks who live on the golf course, also.

Yesterday a busy one. Up early. Stopped at Verizon and Publix. Only one Publix open. Customers looked sad. Heads down, asses dragging. A remnant of Irma?

Also got a haircut, manicure and pedicure.

I was energized all day. Assume it must have been the time I spent at Jean and Joe's. Restful.

Dinner last night with Don and David at Pepi's. One of the few restaurants open. They were only serving off the luncheon menu and did not have all of the items listed. I enjoyed a huge cheeseburger.

The tree in the center of the outside dining room did fall. Big time! Never more to stand. Destroyed part of the roof portion. The roots pulled up half the concrete floor.

One thing bothered me. The FEMA presence in the parking lot on Simonton behind the fire station. Two huge white tents. Took up 2/3's of the parking. Roped off. A couple of hundred people going in and out of the tents signing up for FEMA. Mostly Bahama Village residents. Everyone happy.

Irma and Me

What bothered me were the two Homeland Security guards/officers. Uniformed. Never saw one before.

Tall, thin, crew cut hair, blue uniforms and guns on the hips. Reminded me of the neo-Nazis in Greece I have written about many times.

Their appearance bothered me. I asked myself why does this agency need its own military force.

A fire yesterday. 717 Duval. Reported flames engulfed the building. Fire Department got the fire under control. The building housed a tattoo shop.

Food is a problem. There is scarcity. Monroe County announced free breakfasts and lunches to all school children till October 25.

I compliment Senator Mc Cain on his Obamacare stand.

Two observations.

Google maps. First time I ever used the service. Off my cell phone. Where have I been? Wow!

The *Key West Citizen*. Could be the beginning of the end. The *Citizen* is downsizing. Henceforth the *Citizen* will produce only two editions a week. A weekend edition on Saturday. Another edition on Wednesday. The *Citizen* will also soon be moving its printing to Miami.

Sad. A Key West tradition.

Syracuse/LSU tonight. LSU favored by 23 points. Would like to watch the game, never the less. Jack Flats still closed. Might watch at Don's Place.

I will be doing my Key West Lou Live video on Facebook later this afternoon. A quick few minutes. Interesting dialogue.

Enjoy your day!

IRMA AFTERMATH

Posted on September 24, 2017 by Key West Lou

Irma came, did her thing, and left. She left behind ruination, despair and hope.

How things stand today.

I drove down Duval yesterday. From the Gulf to the Atlantic. Not a pretty sight. Most storefronts and buildings still boarded. Physical damage on a varying scale to some buildings.

The most significant observation was the desolation. Few on the street. Very few. Like death had visited.

The bars are starting to open. Rick's, Sloppy Joe's, Irish Kevin's, the Bull, and Jack Flats. More employees than customers. Except for the gay bars in mid Duval. Bourbon Street and 801. Packed.

There was a FEMA truck on Duval. Handing out food packages. Only the minority community evident.

I mentioned the FEMA sign up tents behind the Simonton fire station yesterday. Only minorities evident there. It appears we have left racial/ethnic groups behind. Same as Katrina. Not in assistance today. Rather in becoming part of the American dream.

A cruise ship coming in today. Why? Key West today not the Key West of yesterday. Key West needs time to recuperate. Downtown looks like hell.

Three more cruise ships expected this week.

Some say we have to get business going again. Bring the cruise ships in! Locals need to work. Rent is due the first of the month. Only one week away.

I spent yesterday afternoon resting. Actually, sleeping. The return drive killed me. Just as the drive

Irma and Me

to Birmingham had. My 82 years very evident in the tiredness I am experiencing.

Hit the Chart Room first last night. First time the Chart Room has been open since Irma.

I was the sixth person to arrive. An hour later when I left, I was the only customer remaining.

Shaun bartending.

Peter Petro manages 40 properties. One is the home I live in. I have been bugging the man ever since Irma was on the horizon. Even now since I have returned. Cleanup time. I am a tenant, not an owner. A wonderful experience!

Peter does his job well, even though I am a bit too anxious at times.

Peter was at the Chart Room when I arrived. With his wife Rebecca who I met for the first time. A nice lady.

Rebecca marries people in Key West. She is a Notary and notaries are permitted to do so. In fact, most marriages performed in Key West are by a Notary such as Rebecca. Rebecca also performs live theater at the Red Barn. She is featured in a show opening next month.

Then to Don's Place to watch the Syracuse/LSU game. Don, David, Stan and Claire there.

Sitting next to me watching the game were Troy and Jenny. Troy a diehard Michigan fan. He was watching Michigan on one screen as I was watching Syracuse on the one next to it.

Syracuse looked good the first half. Gave up 10 points they should not have. Still in the game, however. Syracuse defense played well.

LSU got another touchdown at the beginning of the second half. Syracuse was basically 3 touchdowns behind. I viewed it as the beginning of the end. Went home to bed.

Never even tried to find out the final score till this morning. Syracuse came back. Sort of. Final score had LSU winning 35-26. A late 4th quarter LSU touchdown led to LSU's 35 points.

Syracuse was a 23 point underdog going into the game. Syracuse played well. They did better than LSU stat wise. Note LSU was a ranked team going into the game.

This is not going to be a Syracuse year. Better than most in recent years I suspect. Perhaps glory will return a few years from now. It has been a long time.

Yesterday was the first day Don's was open its full hours.

Ice is a problem all over town. Bar owners and restaurants are running all over looking for some to buy.

Our animal and fish friends are of concern also.

A Sugarloaf homeowner was looking out his window. Thought he saw a porpoise stranded in the mangroves. Called the Sheriff's Office, who in turn contacted Wildlife Conservation and the dolphin hospital Dolphin Plus.

Representatives of all three groups hurried to the scene and effected a rescue. Two veterinarians involved. They waded out to the porpoise. A female. Slightly burned from the sun. Otherwise, ok. Carried her to deeper water and let her go.

I received a red flag call this morning from Jeanne H. Stevenson. Not a Key Wester. Her sister Anne is, however. She can't reach Anne. Concerned. Wants to know if I could help.

Anne sells newspapers outside the church. All I was told about her.

Anyone having any information re Anne, please let me know so I can convey it on to her sister.

Irma and Me

Key West's curfew was lifted yesterday. Stay out all night folks!

The remainder of the Keys still have curfews.

Comcast making progress. A step at a time. Too little from my perspective. I had TV when I returned home last night. Still no landline or wi-fi.

Sloan due soon. A ton of catch-up work to do.

Enjoy your Sunday!

POST IRMA

I am writing this brief Irma update October 15. Roughly three weeks since my last post. I thought you might be interested in how the cleanup is going.

Slowly. Very slowly. So much to be done.

Everyone helping, Neighbors and friends each other. Public facilities. FEMA. First responders. Key West and the lower Keys not being treated like Puerto Rico.

Key West lucked out. Got hit. Not as bad as it could have. Irma swerved at the last minute. Hit Sugarloaf north to Marathon big time. You have seen pictures of Puerto Rico on television. The Sugarloaf-Marathon area looks the same.

Irma's surge hit Key West at low tide. Luckily. Only 2.5 feet. If at high tide later in the day, Wilma all over again.

It struck as a category 4. Significant damage in Key West. Not as bad as Sugarloaf north. Key West lost a ton of trees. I lost 6. One big. Ripped the roots right out of the ground. Tree debris consisting of trees, leaves and bark still rest on the sides of side streets. Both sides. The main thoroughfares cleaned.

The debris non-ending.

It is hot. Every day 85 plus degrees. Rains several times a day. The debris gets wet. The sun returns. The smell/stink overwhelming.

Not all of Duval Street open. Questionable whether Duval will be totally open for Fantasy Fest next week. Some restaurants and bars will not be able to open till after November 1. Some next year. That bad.

Duval Street dead in the evening. Very few visitors.

Irma and Me

Sugarloaf up to Marathon a long time disaster. Too many buildings down. It could take 2-3 years.

The lower Keys will kick back. There is a determination. An impressive determination.

God willing, no more Irmas for a few years.

IRMA AND ME

Gallery

Irma and Me

Louis Petrone

Irma and Me

Louis Petrone

Irma and Me

Irma and Me

Louis Petrone

Irma and Me

Irma and Me

Irma and Me

Irma and Me

Irma and Me

Louis Petrone

Irma and Me

Louis Petrone

Irma and Me

Louis Petrone

Irma and Me

Irma and Me

Acknowledgments

Sloan Kelly is my assistant. No way could I do anything I do without her assistance. That includes this book. We work hand in hand. Thank you, Sloan. Pictures galore. Thanks go to Shaun Ryan, John Holster, Jean Thornton, Heidi Schramm, Corey Malcom, Cyndy and Howard Livingston, Joanne Martin, and Ann Zaler. They are responsible for the pictures in Irma and Me. Thanks also to my fellow evacuees to Birmingham. Ann Zaler, Joanne Martin, Dan Schwab, Hayward McKee, Suzette Kelly, Wil Kinsey, and three dogs. Without them, there would be no story. Last but not least, Jean and Joe Thornton. Our hosts in Birmingham. Two better people do not exist.

About the Author

Louis Petrone was first a successful environmental attorney in New York who maintained a national reputation. He retired to Key West. In retirement, he has blossomed into a blog writer, television and blog talk radio host, a newspaper columnist and writer. All with an international following. Petrone has four children and nine grandchildren.

Petrone does a daily blog read world wide: My Life in Key West. keywestlou.com. And he does a podcast Tuesday nights: Tuesday Talk with Key West Lou. www.blogtalkradio.com/key-west-lou. Also he does a daily video on Facebook: Key West Lou Live.

The New Atlantian Library

NewAtlantianLibrary.com
or AbsolutelyAmazingEbooks.com
or AA-eBooks.com

www.ingramcontent.com/pod-product-compliance
Lightning Source LLC
Chambersburg PA
CBHW070542170426
43200CB00011B/2518